Know Your Relationships

SHILPI J CHAWLA

AF518092

EMBASSY BOOKS
www.embassybooks.in

Know Your Relationships
©Shilpi J Chawla 2017

First Edition 2017

Published in India by:
Embassy Book Distributors
120, Great Western Building,
Maharashtra Chamber of Commerce Lane,
Fort, Mumbai 400 023, India
Tel: (+9122) -30967415, 22819546
Email: info@embassybooks.in
www.embassybooks.in

ISBN: 978-81-933415-2-0

All rights reserved. No part of this publication may be reproduced, distributed, or transmitted in any form or by any means, including photocopying, recording, or other electronic or mechanical methods, without the prior written permission of the publisher. The use of brief quotations embodied in reviews is permitted.

Cover Design by Sonal Churi

Layout and typesetting by PSV Kumarasamy

Printed at Repro Knowledgecast Limited, Thane

Praise for

Know Your Relationships

I recognised your writer's voice: it is the Voice of Spirit.
Your words are Heart Words; they are words that touch the Heart and bring with them, gentle contemplation and Love.
I Bless you for the Gift that you bring to the Hearts and Minds of our World.

-Paul & Neelam Hinsberger,
Shamanic Counselors and Teachers

"Know Your ABC" is a beautiful concept & a must read for mothers.
Your intention" May each of you find something new and extra ordinary in your own choices on a daily basis," has been conveyed very aptly through all the chapters.
My favourite line from the book is : Just relax, all that needs to be taken care of is already done!
This is such an immensely motivating statement.
I am sure this book will help a lot of mothers look at parenting from a different aspect.
Positivity & a true feeling of love is shared through your books.

- Saudamini Sharma,
Director, Gopal Sharma Blooming Buds

This book inspires us to live our day to day challenges with the help of comfortable tools and with a perfect measurement of all 26 ingredients (26 letters) to be used periodically.
It is a complete blend of qualities, hopes, morals, virtues and most importantly instincts that one should have as one embarks on to different journeys of their life.
The 26 ingredients mentioned in the book guides us and makes our sixth sense activated strongly.
I will remember this book for encouraging me to enjoy life by cooking a delicious recipe of living it to the fullest and in the best spirit.

- Meghna Thakkar,
Clinical Psychologist, Play Therapy Practitioner,
Director of Childvilla

Every intention you have expressed cannot have its source other than your heart. There is innocence in your writing and this brings out the child in the reader. Living the ABC's within this book is bound to increase the Emotional Quotient of parents and their children enabling them to prosper in their emotional and social dimensions. Great work!

- Rajeev Mehra,
Founder, The Lighthouse Wellness Studio

A must read for all mothers and fathers. If every parent were to share these intentions and blessings with their children,it would definitely make their lives more joyful.
Bless you Shilpi for spreading love and happiness.

- Anu Mehra,
Founder, The Lighthouse Wellness Studio

~

A Prayer

Dear Spirit...
As I invite the inner guides and invoke their divine energies to flow
with the idea that is the culmination of this book,
I surrender to clear vision so that I may write with Conviction
I pray that the process may be Joyous so that we may
all learn and grow with each new revelation
I connect with my higher self and carry forward
the Willingness to unlearn the past,
such that through the journey of this book,
every child including me may experience
a new way of integrating their
A B C's in relationships

~

Intention

We all have learnt A B C as a child,
I feel it is time to re-create some spark and ignite the way
we recall these letters in the present day and age.
It is my intention to create a fresh and bright perspective
of looking at relationships through the lens of this book.
May the simplicity of this concept inspire us all to
look for RELIEF in the mundane.
I believe in the universal life force energy and
keep the adrenaline rush going as I share my visions and
understandings of living a life that allows
Growth, Gratitude and Greatness.
May each of you find something new and
extra ordinary in your own choices on a daily basis.

~

Gratitude for the StoneHedge

The image on the left is that of a rock in my building garden. During one of our monthly Shamanism class, my teachers energised and charged this rock with the power of Intention. My association with it since, grew to be sacred, as I would visit, talk and feed it on many mornings with incense sticks, water and my presence.
On one particularly contemplative Sunday afternoon, I sat staring at this very rock. I felt like I was beginning to receive a lot of clear guidance and encouragement through my sense perceptions to pen down the book you now hold in your hands,
Know Your Relationships.

The seed was planted and so I decided to be open to the process of Spirit, inspite of the heavy resistance I may have been feeling at the time.
I received some messages and intentions very strongly at that point in time and as a sign of great respect and gratitude towards this rock that I began to lovingly address as StoneHedge, I am sharing them here.

The StoneHedge said,

Hold the intention to be a mother to all, only because you can, it is not you who gives, it is the earth. In simple words this would mean, to hold the intention to love all.

To care enough to come back. Caring is good but to care enough is a step further. It opens up possibilities for unconditional love and support.

To be empty and yet know that it is okay to feel nothing. Being comfortable with the void is a sign of deep love for life.

To allow the cry of emotion to soothe your soul , to know emotion is to know life.

Resources are a house of treasure, therefore share information as it brings blessings to all

~

Blessings

The right page of every chapter is filled with blessings for relationships.

You may want to know,
What is a blessing?

A blessing requires you to search your heart and pour out the love that is contained within it in the form of a note to the other.
Wishing someone well is all it takes at the core to really get the blessing moving forward.

The reason each chapter is supported by a blessing is to enhance ones ability to sense and feel the connection to their own heart and therefore to all of life including other individuals.
After all we are all created from the same Divine Spark!

~

Why this book?

As I started to get my twin boys ready for the process of
schooling, I realised I had to first get ready to
show up in class myself.
The secure environment indoors felt this huge
blow as there was a need to now open a new doorway and
let go of my children into a world that meant, outside.

I wanted to protect myself and a lot more of them from the
unknown that was going to meet us through the changed
routines, scheduled timings and new interactions.
As my heart began to sink, I noticed this urge
in me to validate all that I was feeling through my writings.

A book just restating my intentions for the children was
an idea that was planted in my heart.
Very soon, my mind drove in to play the role
of an ally as it enabled me to see how the
information produced here can be used
as a universal way for people across the planet
to declare and set their intentions into motion towards
every relationship in their life, including self.

So here I am, cheerfully embracing the new change
in my life with a redefined version of A B C.
There were moments when
I questioned myself if I was to pen down
all of the amazing stuff in the way
that it was flowing and yet,
somewhere I already knew it had to be done.

I thank my readers for staying open to
new possibilities and ideas.

May you find new meaning to your
Relationships through the journey of the pages ahead.

~

How to use this book?

Regular reading : The book can be read page by page to receive inspiration and delve into a new perspective towards relationships.

Declaring your intentions as a parent : Pick up a letter of your choice and read through the
details pertaining to that specific letter.
You must FEEL the sync as you connect the words in the book, with the power of your thoughts, feelings and actions.
The question that would be most relevant to ask here is,
What can I give to this relationship with my child?
There is bound to be a connection between the question you ask and the answer you receive.

For example, if I thought of my children and put forth the question, What can I give to this relationship?
I might then think of a letter that comes to my awareness.
In this case, my letter being Q. I glance through
the text forQ, Q stands for questions as per the chapter heading in this book.

As I read through I am drawn to understand and empathise with my role as a Mother towards my children.
The entire quote on Questions instantly helps me to calm down and embrace the uncertainty of being perfect.

Universal aid to set intentions for loved ones
across all relationships : the intentions and affirmations written for each letter can be used freely for any relationship that is of significance to you at this point in your life.
The question that would be most relevant to ask then is,
What can I give to this relationship?
There is bound to be a connection between the question you ask and the answer you receive.

For example, if I thought of my relationship with my sister and put forth the question, What can I give to this relationship?
I might then think of a letter that comes to my awareness.
In this case, my letter being A.
I glance through the text for A, A stands for allow
as per the chapter heading in this book.

Every line is now making sense and coming alive guiding me to be more allowing of her ways of being.
I am drawn to think of the joy that sparkles through her eyes and the awe she expresses in simple living.
I feel a sense of spaciousness within, almost like an expansion of my heart.

Please note, you must Read between the lines and ensure your knowing takes precedence over your thinking.

Stay IN-SPIRED!

Stay TRUE- to-WHO YOU ARE!

~

Dedication

This book is an epitome of love for my husband and twin boys.
Thank you BOYS!

Index

- A for allow
- B for bliss
- C for courage
- D for dream
- E for expectation
- F for fun
- G for gut
- H for home
- I for inspiration

- J for joy
- K for kind
- L for love
- M for mother
- N for nothing
- O for opportunities
- P for play
- Q for questions
- R for rest
- S for sing

- T for trust
- U for understand
- V for victory
- W for water
- X for xylophone
- Y for yes
- Z for zest

A for ALLOW

Allow : it is my intention to allow your giggles to guide me.
I allow the awe & wonder in your eyes to be
the centre of my focus.

I allow you to be free

I allow you to be happy

I allow you to explore

I allow you your world of carefree days

I allow myself to learn to be joyous just like you

I allow the child in me to play with the child that is you

I allow our pure connection to thrive and grow

And as it does I allow me to
align with the brilliance that is US.

A for ALLOW

A blessing towards this relationship

I bless your arms to be open, always

I bless your embrace be true, encapsulated with immense love

I bless your gestures be genuine and graceful

I bless your eyes witness deep love and understanding

I bless you attract your relationships of unconditional love and warm support

B for BLISS

Bliss : Seeing and Sensing the blessing that you are, is experiencing bliss in many moments. It is my intention to feel blissful all through our journey together

Bliss is for real

To watch your smile go into your eyes is Blissful

To hold your fingers and feel them intertwine with mine is Blissful

You are proof of that LIVE bliss each day of the year

As you grow in all ways, be the bliss that you are internally

May I never forget this magical essence you came with

May you only know bliss as your true identity

Be blissfully you, Be happy!

B for BLISS

A blessing towards this relationship

I bless your eyes to see beyond what lies at the surface

I bless your gaze rest on all things profound

I bless your space glow with lights and
match the many moods you experience

I bless you to envision the simplicity in all that
may seem complex

I bless you to radiate blissfully bright each day

C for COURAGE

Courage : it is my intention to inspire you by example
therefore I share my stories with conviction and care.

Care for the beating heart

Care to feel your smile

Care to give love

Care to care only because you can

I am courageous and I radiate that energy to you
in my interactions

You are courageous and I already know that, about you

May the capacity within you to sow the seed of
unconditional love be the centre of all that you create.

C for COURAGE

A blessing towards this relationship

I bless you to carry yourself up with confidence

I bless you to create only because you care to

I bless you to respect your lows and
stay grounded in your highs

I bless you to look through all the concerns and conflicts

I bless you to be the cause

D for Dream

Dream : It is my intention to stay open and hold space as you weave your imagination and dream your dreams

Be a dreamer all through life

Life is more fun than you can begin to imagine

I honour every dream you share

I have immense respect for your ability to express yourself

May the universe conspire to work through all details so that the dreamer in you begins to take flight..

Dust off the doubts

Dare to dream
and know that you deserve to be Happy.

D for Dream

A blessing towards this relationship

I bless you to many possibilities

I bless you to explore your potential

I bless you to weave your magic at your own terms

I bless you to fulfilling and satisfying resources

I bless you to dream big

E for Expectation

Expectation : It is my intention to expect the best for us.

I sense that at every step as the path unfolds,
you are filled with the expectation of
enthusiasm and excitement to meet life.

I expect us to be the perfect family

I expect you to keep up healthy

I expect us to be on the same page as far as wellbeing goes

I expect that you will meet many mirrors
along the way and that you will cultivate
responsibility to look them all in the eye with respect

I expect us to embrace our uniqueness as
individuals and collectively as a family

I expect to love you in new ways each day of the year

E for Expectation

A blessing towards this relationship

I bless you to have healthy expectations

I bless you expect to receive unconditionally

I bless you to make decisions expecting them to work out for all

I bless you to value your own presence

I bless you to treasure relationships

F for Fun

Fun : it is my intention to forget everything and instead follow your fun ways.

I watch you as you play

I follow your lead and we all enjoy

Life was always supposed to be fun

May I continue to reinforce this simple message as we are together

May you grow in age, but never forget the spirit with which you played all the games

You innocence is admirable, Your smiles are precious

So let us meet once again and recreate the moments just for fun.

F for Fun

A blessing towards this relationship

I bless you to find humour in most things that life presents

I bless you to laugh your heart out when you need to

I bless you to connections that match your wavelength

I bless you find joy in little moments

I bless you have your fun, your way.

G for GUT

Gut : it is my intention to go for my gut feeling every time. I know you pick on this way of living as we share the same space.

We are connected

I honour our time together and therefore am aware of how I behave around you

We are guided in each day of our lives with a pulsating throbbing feeling in the stomach

I want you to know that you are never alone even if no one seems to be around

Go with your gut and you will cross all tests with flying colours

Get inside you and you will feel that you are along the right way, for you

Let your gut take over and you will never look to another for your answers.

G for GUT

A blessing towards this relationship

I bless you stay grounded, firm and secure in your roots

I bless you get into your space often

I bless you get ready to greet every sunrise with a smile

I bless you believe in the goodness that life holds
in every cell of your body

I bless you get set and go for your gut each time.

H for HOME

Home: it is my intention to make our house into a home.
A heaven for rest, comfort, peace and love.

Home is the best place on earth

We can be home wherever we go

All you got to be is Comfortable in your OWN skin

The world is full of goodness

The universe has your back

Trust your instincts

Make your decisions in your time

For, you are always home in your heart

H for HOME

A blessing towards this relationship

I bless our home with laughter, love and peace

I bless our home with abundance, joy and prosperity

I bless your footsteps be guided in the right direction each time you leave home

I bless your ability to be comfortable

I bless you to feel safe and surrender to Divine Will.

I for INSPIRATION

Inspiration: it is my intention to create out of inspired-action. May your actions be the basis of your inspired thoughts each time.

Daily living is sacred

Life happens in the moments and I want us to stay inspired

Explore the same things again

Enjoy the sounds of the flying plane

Sense through nature and create your own connections

Know that you are beyond your achievements and your last name

You are a living miracle

Your presence has inspired me to be a better person

May OUR connection continue to fuel this sense of being such that you may 'do' only when truly inspired.

I for INSPIRATION

A blessing towards this relationship

I bless you enjoy inspiration through all of your senses

I bless you satisfaction of the highest degree in all that you choose to do

I bless you find value in inspiring conversations

I bless you to enjoy your own company

I bless you to be an inspiration first to yourself and then others

J for JOY

Joy : I take responsibility for my happiness, you take responsibility for yours. It is my intention that we count on the unlimited positive energy within our own system to move forward with joy.

Just you, Just your vibe

Just know you own your energy

Just be the joy that you naturally are, Just chill out more on your own

Just relax, all that needs to be taken care of is already done

Just be ready for the day before you wake up

Show up with a smile because you are complete and an absolute joy to be around.

J for JOY

A blessing towards this relationship

I bless you to discern with joy

I bless you to healthy choices

I bless you to vibrations that soothe your soul

I bless you to see your reality inside out

I bless you to infectious smiles

K for KIND

Kind : Your noble thoughts towards all are so pure and uncensored by the judgement of conditions. It is my intention to continue to stay open and learn through you.

You are the kind who owes your mind the peace that goes beyond understanding

You are the kind who owes your spirit the gentle caress

You are the kind who owes your body gratitude

Kindness will always be subtle and therefore very crucial

Kind in action is equal to Kind in Spirit

I sense you extending the kindness that comes from your soul towards all

And in those moments I bow down to you in great respect and love

K for KIND

A blessing towards this relationship

I bless you to the kind attention of teachers and gurus

I bless you to be kind like a king

I bless the kindred soul that you are

I bless your actions to be the basis of kind and informed choices

I bless you to look at the bigger picture, always

L for LOVE

Love : I intend to love you unconditionally. May you know that this is the only way of truly loving anything or anyone in your life.

Love can set us free

Love is going to be our approach

You choose me because you knew how important love is in its raw essence

Love allows us to give

Love comes from a heart that is full

And your heart is complete in all ways

I know you can express love

I know you are capable of receiving and yet giving is what love expects of us all

Therefore give
Give with the intention and awareness that you are full

Give because you don't want anything from anyone

Give because you are abundant in Consciousness.

L for LOVE

A blessing towards this relationship

I bless you to be re-charged with love that is
in your own heart

I bless you to know the true language of love

I bless you to respect your boundaries

I bless us to love each other beyond conditions

I bless you to love all

M for MOTHER

Mother : it is my intention to highlight the power and grace of our true provider, our real mother, Mother Earth.

Yes, I am your Mother

Yes, I love you immensely

Yes, I know I will do my best

And yet, I want you to know that there is a Divine Mother who is the ultimate nurturer.

She gives like none other,

She knows you like no one could ever understand

She guides us all , therefore remember to pay your respects and offer gratitude for her gentle gaze on you at all times

M for MOTHER

A blessing towards this relationship

I bless you to be nurtured by the strength of the wind

I bless you to be nourished by the compassion of the water

I bless you to mull over higher truths coming from the mountains

I bless you to movement that stretches and soothes your stride, like the sun

I bless you to wellbeing within the mind-body-soul

N for NOTHING

Nothing - If you can be pleased by doing nothing,
you own everything. It is my intention to
introduce this 'space' to us.

No thing can be a source of happiness

No person can ever complete you

Nothingness is a state of being okay with everything

Know that nothing can be taken away from you

I pray that you may receive a sense of fulfilment in
the zone of doing nothing many times in your day

You came from nothingness,
And that's our ultimate destination

So let's do nothing and yet have a blast together!

N for NOTHING

A blessing towards this relationship

I bless us to the zero zone of nothingness

I bless you to do nothing and yet be fulfilled with everything

I bless you to witness nature in all its moods

I bless you to know your own inner nature

I bless you to co-create with the universe from
a space of nothingness.

O for OPPORTUNITIES

Opportunities : it is my intention to look at each day spent with you as an opportunity to see life through a brand new lens.

Oh my god, you are finally here

Your presence has crafted so much giving within us

May you live many days of your life knowing that life is an opportunity you choose

And, you choose well

The world is safe and here to serve you

Share easily, Slow down.
and each day let the impeccable timing of
this planet delight you

O for OPPORTUNITIES

A blessing towards this relationship

I bless you to see each day as an opportunity to explore

I bless you to become friends with time

I bless you to be present to the rhythm of your breath

I bless you to watch the rains and reflect on silently

I bless you to know that every choice you make is an opportunity

P for PLAY

Play : I feel the palpable pulsating energy as I watch you play.
You are so alive and alert, it is my intention to give
the child in me permission to play along with you.

Let us play together

I want to give you all the attention and yet play easy

I sense your enthusiasm as you play with such comfort

You are a player, all heart and pure

Believe in your game

Balance the old and new

Create boundaries and yet know your ability to
stretch can be a playful act.

P for PLAY

A blessing towards this relationship

I bless you to create your own game

I bless you to be a game changer

I bless you to know the rules and yet be willing to go beyond

I bless you to play irrespective of the age you are at

I bless you to set your boundaries as you play along

Q for QUESTIONS

Questions : It is my intention to help us to stay in awe of the questions for they bring creativity and add a new dimension to our growth.

I want you to know that it is okay to have a question unanswered

It is okay to ask a question twice

It is okay if you take time to understand

The best question you will ever ask is Who Am I ?

The most profound answer you will ever receive will be your own

You can never go wrong

So take your time as you frame your questions

And embrace the uncertainty of it being answered immediately

Q for QUESTIONS

A blessing towards this relationship

I bless you to find your peace with uncertainty

I bless you to know your answers

I bless you to ask for what you want

I bless you to substitute waiting with stillness

I bless you to be comfortable in your own skin

R for REST

Rest : It is my intention to learn to rest like the way you do. Resting is productive and brings freshness to the same day in a brand new way.

Read the signs of your body

Give it rest when it needs

Resting preserves your energy

Napping is great for health

Feel the warmth of the bed you lay in

Snuggle into the gentle embrace of your own hands

Rest and feel your breath

If you know how to relax, you know how to live.

R for REST

A blessing towards this relationship

I bless you to unwind first thing in the morning

I bless you to be willing to unlearn

I bless you to process and please yourself first

I bless you to focus on the journey in-between
the beginning and end

I bless every gaze that rests on you come from a space of love

S for SING

Sing : it is my intention to sing along as i go, it soothes my soul.
I know you hear me and stay open to your tunes.

Songs are for your soul

Sing along your favourite ones to move in ways
you didn't know you could

Everything comes into harmony when you hum from the heart

May you sing many songs of love with great passion

May you brighten your mornings with the melody
of your own voice

May you use the power of music to move
through the many choices

And sing through life at your volume,
knowing that those who watch you, do so with love.

S for SING

A blessing towards this relationship

I bless you to search your soul and find the path of doing so extremely rewarding

I bless you to let your voice be audible

I bless you to sing your song with such conviction

I bless you to stay connected to your inner being

I bless you to emote all the way through

T for TRUST

Trust: I trust the process of life. It is my intention to invite an attitude of surrender and gratitude in all of our days ahead.

Life is full of good people and high intentions

Trust the connections you make

Trust the sunsets you see to motivate you to start another day with vigour and energy

Trust the clouds to tell you a new story each day

Trust your body with all its messages

Trust that a power beyond your comprehension has your back

Trust that you are very loved for no reason,
Except that you exist!

T for TRUST

A blessing towards this relationship

I bless you to treat people well

I bless you to relationships of gold

I bless you to try something new every now and then

I bless you to give your commitment and time to that which centres you

I bless you to shine the brightest in every forum of life

U for UNDERSTAND

Understand : it is my intention to honour and encourage you for as much as you are willing to understand at any given point.

You understand so much which is so amazing

I want to understand you more

As you merge with the new learnings one day at a time, you will rise

Your pace is perfect

Your stance is admirable

Your gaze is full of smiles

May you respect the innocence in understanding self such that you would never have to make any efforts towards understand another.

U for UNDERSTAND

A blessing towards this relationship

I bless you to care for how you feel

I bless you to communicate clearly

I bless you to get back up and clear the dust off the past

I bless you to be guided at every juncture

I bless us to understand each other all the way

V for VICTORY

Victory : it is my intention to beat the drum
of your success in your ears.

You are a true winner!

Each day counts cause you have woken up and
are Alive to it

Each day you create something new

Each day you give us an opportunity to love

Your physical presence in our world is a victory for us

May you see yourself as important

May you know success before it appears

May you contemplate where you came from

And in that, may you enjoy the authority of being a true
winner.

V for VICTORY

A blessing towards this relationship

I bless you to expand your horizons

I bless that you may serve with compassion and care

I bless you continue to sense the highly important agenda
you have here

I bless you to see your strengths with gratitude
and your weaknesses with grace

I bless you to play your game like a winner

W for WATER

Water : The wind, the sun, the water, this earth are all here with you as you establish your connection with them.
It is my intention to allow nature to steer our relationship at every turn.

You are as pure as the crystals of water

You are filled with clarity cause your thoughts are focused

Your ability to move forward is enhanced
through the consumption of water

Water brings us healing, emotionally

May you learn to accept your emotions and know
that while change is inevitable,
it is beautiful and you are safe through the process

Count on the element of water to keep you calm
as you carry on.

W for WATER

A blessing towards this relationship

I bless you to bond with nature like a best friend

I bless you to create heaven on earth

I bless you to allow change as you stand in your power

I bless you to create high flying concierge in the clouds

I bless you to be free like the bird in the sky

X for XYLOPHONE

Xylophone : the sweet sound of music is like
solace to the soul. I intend to keep our journey high in
vibration through the many different tunes and moods we
may experience.

You like music, I see how it fills you up.

Choose your instrument, Play your song

Let the beats be loud

May you find your energy renewed as
you discover new genres

I pray that you are vocal about your preferences

I pray that you may be comfortable being visible
in all your glory

May the gift of music bring peace to your soul,
joy to your heart and
love to this world.

X for XYLOPHONE

A blessing towards this relationship

I bless the spirit in you to reach out

I bless the voice in your throat be bold

I bless your eyes sparkle with awe as you savour
your favourite tune

I bless you to swallow all the goodness
that you want to experience

I bless that the spirit in all of the instruments
teach you their melody

Y for Yes

Yes : I intend to affirm my Yes to a happy life experience. You are born in a Yes universe and your Yes counts.

Yes, you are here

Yes, I love you

Yes, you owe nothing to no one

Yes, you are the best thing that happened to this planet

Yes, your presence makes a difference

Yes, your smile is the most gratifying experience

Yes, you are going to have such a good life

May you say Yes to every enriching, exciting, enlightening experience.

Y for Yes

A blessing towards this relationship

I bless you with affirmations that serve you

I bless you to say Yes to the ever lasting companionship
you will discover with this universe

I bless you to say Yes to yourself first

I bless you to allow all of the resources that this planet has,
to line up for you.

Z for Zest

Zest : I intend to keep our will to be alive and live an extra delicious experience a priority at all times.

I sense your zeal for life

It is infectious and extremely welcoming

I share your passion for new connections

I adore the energy with which you greet every sunrise

Your decisions radiate maturity as you act through wisdom

The energy that is the source of all,
is within you and me

May your zeal be enough to move mountains
and create the everlasting willingness to be more of you

Z for Zest

A blessing towards this relationship

I bless your enthusiasm and high energy

I bless your intentions give you direction

I bless your prayers bring you peace

I bless your pace be perfect for you

I bless you till eternity

Few words for my BOYS, my Inspiration

I am always in love with YOU

I admire your innocence

I know your smile

I care for your ways

I am always in love with who you are

I want to hold you

I want to stop you, before you fall

I want the best, perhaps the bestest for you

I am constantly contemplating new ways of enjoying you

I am always in love with who you are

My heart feels full and yet it is empty

I know you will grow up in new ways

But my love knows no limits

You are the star I see

You are the moon and sun that is my universe

I am always rising in my heart to meet you

I am always in love with who you are

~

Thank you to my readers

Love is the real thing

May we find it in our own hearts FIRST

May we be full with its power

May we all extend it out to our children and families

Knowing that in the giving, there is abundance

Knowing that in the giving, there is peace

Knowing that in me-is YOU!

~

Other Titles from this Author

For more deatils visit

www.shilpichawlabooks.com

~